# S is for Sentence

Thomas E. Simmons

# S is for Sentence

*or*

*The Virgin at the End of this Book*

~

*starring lovable, furry old*

*Thomas E. Simmons*

~

*Hello everybody![1]*

---

[1] Thomas E. Simmons (b. 1967).

*Wait a minute –*

*What did that say?*


*On that last page –*


*Did it say there will be a virgin at the end of this book?*


*IT DID?*


*Listen, I have an idea:*


*If you do not turn any pages, we will never get to the end of this book*

*You turned the page!*

*He looks grouchy*

---

[2] (1516-1590).

# Table of Contents

*You could put down the book now*

*You could just stop right here*

*It's your choice*

*Let's not be unreasonable*

*Acknowledgements*

Grateful acknowledgements are extended to the editors of the publications where the following poems (or earlier versions of them) in this volume first appeared:

*xiv* as "Tardigrade Physiology" in THE SHOWBEAR FAMILY CIRCUS

*xxi* as "exspiro" in THE WRITE LAUNCH

*xxx* as "Deuel County Flocks" in SOUTH DAKOTA MAGAZINE

*xl* as "Mycophagy" in AROMATICA POETICA

*xlviii* as "That Chicken Heart Which Consumed the World" in THIRTEEN MYNA BIRDS

*xliv* as "A Tax Thicket: 26 U.S.C. §§" in NORTH DAKOTA QUARTERLY


Dürer and Thévet drawings reproduced pursuant to a license from Alamy.


*That was nice of them!*

Thomas E. Simmons is a lawyer, a lifelong South Dakotan (so long as one does not count a few years in Canada, one in Japan, and a handful in Nebraska), and a tenured professor at the University of South Dakota's Knudson School of Law in Vermillion, South Dakota (USA). He serves as the faculty advisor for the Saint Thomas More Society and teaches courses such as Estate Planning, Trusts & Wills, Remedies in Law and Equity, and Professional Responsibility. His scholarship follows those same topics. He is a fellow of the American College of Tax Counsel and a scholar with the speaker's bureau of the South Dakota Humanities Council. He serves as an Associate Justice for the Rosebud Sioux Tribe Supreme Court and he is a member of the South Dakota Advisory Committee to the U.S. Commission on Civil Rights.

Tom manages a modest creative output of criticism and poetry. *Loose-Leaf Tod Browning Encyclopedia* (Cyberwit 2020) is his biographical collection of poems and hybrid pieces considering the life and cinematic creations of American director Tod Browning (who helped create films like *Freaks*, *Dracula*, and *The Virgin of Stamboul*, as well as a number of Lon Chaney silent pictures).

*About the Illustrator*

Yasemin Arkun is a professional freelance artist who resides in Istanbul, Turkey. After graduating with a degree in architecture, she worked as a 3-D visualization artist and designer in architectural offices and also as a freelancer. Despite her busy schedule as an architect, she kept on her career as a painter. Since 2017, she has been a full-time freelance artist.

She works in various mediums – graphite, watercolor, acrylic, oil, et cetera. Besides portrait commissions and various works, she has illustrated several children's books.

*Thank you, Ms. Arkun!*

Most church historians and theologians know Peter Lombard as just that – Peter Lombard. Most other folks have never heard of him. But he has other names that are not infrequently bandied about by those few that do, such as Pierre Lombard, Peter the Lombard, Petrus Lombardus, my personal favorite, Petri Lombardi, or simply *L–*.

As his name suggests, *L–* was Italian. Many other details remain obscure. It is said that he was born in a rural commune in Piedmont under the family name of Lumellogno, but among the more cautious historians, even this is disputed. His family was probably poor.[3] Even today, Lumellogno has a population of only about 1,500. It is bounded by rice paddy fields on one side and a tributary of the Po[4] called Agògna (which might be good for leisurely canoe trips when the spring thaw adds to its modest ripples) on the other.

Although *L–*'s family likely was without riches and his probable commune lacked importance, he went on to become a teacher at the esteemed cathedral school of Notre Dame. There, he met leading

---

[3] North Americans tend to believe they have a monopoly on the Horatio Alger rags-to-riches (or even, in *L–*'s case, rags-to-bishopric) biographies; that only U.S. residents can secure promotions by means of pulling themselves up by the bootstraps. This assumption is erroneous. The widespread availability of bootstraps is in fact a global phenomenon.

[4] Not to be confused with the Tellytubby voiced by Piu Fan Lee.

theologians Peter Abelard and Hugh of Saint Victor. Before long, *L–* became a celebrated theologian in his own right. By about 1145, he had been promoted to the position of magister (a professor, essentially) at the Notre Dame school. His impressive teaching and lively intellect soon caught the attention of his students and superiors.

So, two years later, he became a subdeacon. Three years after that, he rose to the rank of deacon, and after another two years, archdeacon. Deacons where not then ordained members of the clergy, but in 1156 or thereabouts, *L–* was ordained and entered the priesthood. Then in 1159, he was consecrated the bishop of Paris. Sadly, in less than a year, he was dead, at the age of perhaps sixty.

Today, *L–*'s tomb cannot be found by tourists visiting the Cathedral of Notre Dame because the cathedral's construction was not commenced until after his death – not too long after his death – by his successor, Maurice de Sully. Instead, *L–*'s tomb was placed in the church of Saint-Marcel. (Saint Marcel[5] (c. 396-436) was the ninth bishop of Paris). A transcription of the tomb's epitaph (reciting *L–*'s authorship of commentaries and *The Sentences*) survives, but his tomb does not. During the French Revolution, it was destroyed.

---

[5] During Saint Marcel's tenure, a dragon became habituated to devouring certain Parisian women of ill repute. Saint Marcel dispatched it with his crozier, dispatching the dragon's habit along with it, as part of the bargain. See also *infra* poem *x*.

Similarly, there is an archeological empty space in respect to the administrative accomplishments of *L–* because he left behind very few episcopal *acta*. Not much has survived of *L–*'s agenda, his accomplishments, or his leadership style during his truncated term as bishop. By contrast, he left behind thick, rich, detailed theological texts including his sermons, glosses on Pauline letters and commentaries on the Psalms. But his most notable work by far was the *Libri Quattuor Sententiarum* – a four-volume treatise/compilation popularly known as *The Sentences – The Book of Sentences* – or, later, *The Sentences of Peter Lombard*.[6] Its Book I explicates the Trinity and the unity of God, Book II, creation, Book III, Jesus Christ, and Book IV (titled "The Doctrine of Signs"), the sacraments and the four last things – death, judgment, heaven, and hell.

*The Sentences* is a sort of 12th century encyclopedia which undertakes a systemization of theology,

---

[6] *Sententiae* is the Latin nominative plural of the word *sententia*, meaning short moral sayings (e.g., maxims). See Aristotle, *Rhetoric* 2.21 ("a maxim is a statement, not however concerning particulars … but general; it does not even deal with all general things, as for instance that the straight is the opposite of the crooked, but with the objects of human actions, and with what should be chosen or avoided with reference to them."). In *Hamlet*, Polonius' silly grocery-list compilation of recommendations to Laertes models the technique of sententious speech ("Give every man thy ear, but few thy voice / Take each man's censure, but reserve thy judgment. / Costly thy habit as thy purse can buy, / But not express'd in fancy; rich, not gaudy;" etc.).

something that had not truly been undertaken up to that time. It had an unparalleled lifespan as a college textbook lasting until the 16<sup>th</sup> century.

*L–*'s influence was gigantic. *The Sentences* constructed a sturdy framework and centuries of interpretation was layered upon it. John Calvin quoted *L–* a hundred times in *Institutes of the Christian Religion*. *L–* is quoted frequently in the works of Martin Luther (who as a young man wrote glosses on *The Sentences*), Albert the Great, William of Ockham, Gabriel Biel, and Thomas Aquinas (in whose works I was first was introduced to *L–*). The Bishop, in turn, relied on those theologian-giants who came before him, especially Saint Augustine of Hippo.

I think that it is fair to assert that *L–* is the single most important historical personage of whom almost no one has ever heard.

*The Sentences* outlined a structure for inquiry as well as setting limits on theological inquiry. One of *L–*'s contributions was to link charity with the Holy Spirit. *L–* argued that something divine occurs when an individual loves another human being – or God – the individual's love is *itself* God; the love of one's neighbor participates in the divine and the Trinity.[7] While this is an interesting idea, it has never been officially endorsed by the Catholic Church.

---

[7] See also Saint Augustine, *De Trinitate*, VIII (asserting: "If you see charity, you see the Trinity").

In his first encyclical *Deus caritas est* (2005), Pope Benedict XVI clarified:

> [T]here is a certain *relationship*[8] between love and the Divine: love promises infinity, eternity—a reality far greater and totally other than our everyday existence...

> The epicure Gassendi used to offer Descartes the humorous greeting: "O Soul!" And Descartes would reply: "O Flesh!". Yet it is neither the spirit alone nor the body alone that loves: it is man, the person, a unified creature composed of body and soul, who loves. Only when both dimensions are truly united, does man attain his full stature.

Another influential bit of dogma from *The Sentences* is contained within *L*–'s theory of the sacrament of marriage. Parting with Gratian, *L*– asserted that marriage is formed upon a couple's reciprocal consent. Therefore, consummation is, strictly speaking, unnecessary to complete the sacrament and form an indissoluble union.

Still another theological tidbit is the way in which *L*– characterized the Holy Spirit as gift. We might be familiar with the *procession* of the Holy Spirit; that it proceeds from the Father and the Son. But to say

---

[8] Emphasis supplied.

"love proceeds" seem to lack what *L–* captures by emphasizing that the Holy Spirit is a gift; that third person of the trinity is a gift which is given.

In this collection, I begin with the first actual sentence (following *L–*'s prologue) of Book I of *The Sentences*.

It reads:

> All teaching concerns things or signs.[9]

I have remodeled it – only slightly – (to "Every doctrine springs either / from a thing / or from a sign.").

The second sentence of Book I of the Bishop's *The Sentences* re-emphasizes the first.

It reads:

> With diligent investigation, we have pondered over and over again the contents of the Old and New Law; by God's prevenient grace, it has become clear to us that the study of the sacred page is principally concerned with things or with signs.[10]

---

[9] From Giulio Silano's translation (vol. I).

[10] Ibid. *L–* next quotes Saint Augustine's *On Christian Doctrine* and its assertion that "all teaching is either about things or about signs. But even things are learned through signs. 'Things' here

But I have imagined a new second sentence; a rather long one.

It begins with two words: "Compared to –". The introductory subordinate clause of the second sentence occupies these two words and most of the remaining pages of this simple book of satire, rock and roll, faith, melodrama, wonder, pasticcio, and parody.

The second sentence concludes at the end thereof, naturally enough. The second sentence's concluding subject and its predicate are found on the final page of this poem. This poem therefore occupies two sentences; the first, an ordinary one, and the second, a most unusually long one.[11] Long but not infinite, although that is the effect I would like to impart; something which seems to go on and on; pinwheel-like, spiraling like $L$– pondering "over and over again" the contents of the law.[12] I would like to suggest a kind of participation in the infinite; an infinite of both immensity and of divisibility.

---

properly designates whatever is not used to designate something; but 'signs' designates whatever is used in signifying." Ibid.

[11] This is consistent with some commentators who refer to $L$–'s four thick volumes of theology as four sentences.

[12] See *supra* text accompanying note 10.

An overly verbose speaker we might call a blow-hard; windy. And I hope you might find some wind in the second sentence hereof; a breath; some free torque for the sails. As Saint Thomas Aquinas says, "The differences of things are infinite, so to speak; not infinite in reality but to us."[13]

Our world seems composed, perhaps exclusively, of the finite. Certainly, time is not infinite. Nor is space, nor the capacity of human ambition, nor our capacity for pain, etc. There can loads and loads and loads of any given thing (and this seems to me the subject of the majority of poems written today) but never an infinite load. In this material world, participation in the infinite can be elusive.

A distinction ought to be inserted here. For example, if we are asked when we would consider supporting the latest political fad, we might reply, "When hell freezes over" or "When pigs fly."[14] These are events

---

[13] THOMAS AQUINAS, COMMENTARY ON THE METAPHYSICS OF ARISTOTLE, Book 3, Lesson 8. See also, e.g., PETER A. REDPATH, II A NOT-SO-ELEMENTARY CHRISTIAN METAPHYSICS: AN INTRODUCTION TO RAGAMUFFIN THOMISM 63 (2010) ("Science, philosophy, must study a finite multitude."); ibid. at 55 ("St. Thomas claims that because, to some extent, at least in its existence and having some unity, every effect reflects at least a trace of its cause, some similarity of proportion, a proportionality, exists between finite, created beings and an infinite creator").

[14] My personal favorite colorful infinite/long-finite ambiguity phrase is one which I overheard in a bar surrounded by sagebrush in Montana. The tavern served only two choices for thirsty patrons: Pabst Blue Ribbon and Guinness (both on tap).

which may occur in the future. Their occurrence is indefinite. The time before which they will occur is *potentially* infinite. Thus, this refers to something neither infinite nor finite. If the event occurs (pigs flying, let's say), then it will be presumably far, far in the future. Or it may never happen. If we stretch the highway into the future far enough, we may observe a time when pigs fly – in finite time. Or we may not. It's either never (i.e., infinitely never) or something awfully far in the future.

Time had a beginning point some 14 billion years ago. Christians and many other faithful believe in an end times when time will come to a natural conclusion. The infinitely old or the infinitely large seem absent in the material world.[15] Time has a

---

A fellow patron spouting a moustache modeled after the sagebrush in the area replied to some obscure personal question which called for an infinite/long-finite ambiguity (such as, "When are you planning to fix that fender on your truck?") thusly: "When Captain Kangaroo's hairstyle comes back into style." That might be an infinite stretching in *both* directions – or it might terminate at one end and not the other – *or* it might boast a terminus at both ends since I suppose it is at least possible that the odd mop of Robert James Keeshan (1927-2004) was once stylish in some camps and might be again one day. Fashion does tend to be cyclical. The old mop's loose structure mimicked that of the *Captain Kangaroo* television series (1955-1984) in which it was featured.

[15] God, by contrast, is infinitely good. Perhaps God is infinite in the mathematical sense, but more likely, God is only mathematically infinite analogically speaking. The infinite goodness of God is a sacred mystery. Moreover, God is not of a species, so his infiniteness – a theological infiniteness if you will – is likely not of the same species as mathematical infinity,

terminus on both ends. Except that, as I hinted above, there is also a second variety of the mathematically infinite: the infinitely small and the infinitely divisible.

The typical example of the infinitely small involves an individual who is six inches (.5 foot) away from summiting Mount Everest.[16] Baby steps, getting smaller. He traverses half that distance (3 inches). Then he traverses half that distance (1½ inches), then he traverses half that distance (3/4 of an inch), etc. Stated mathematically (in foot units):

.5, .25, .125, .0625, .03125, .015625…

The individual will never reach Everest's summit, even if he takes an infinite number of steps.[17] Infinity proceeds in an infinite shrinking and diminishing. Thus, take a simple two-letter word like "of" and consider the distance between the "o" and the "f."

---

either. See Jill Le Blanc, *Infinity in Theology and Mathematics*, 29 RELIGIOUS STUDIES 51 (1993).

[16] Britton Keeshan, Captain Kangaroo's grandson, buried a photograph of himself and the Captain at the summit of Mount Everest in 2004.

[17] There were unsubstantiated rumors floating around the internet for a short period that Daniel Day-Lewis, after viewing *A Beautiful Day in the Neighborhood* (TriStar Pictures 2019), was so inspired by Tom Hanks' performance as Fred Rogers, that Day-Lewis explored an option by which he would come out of retirement and play the starring role in a biographical drama film of the life of Captain Kangaroo.

We can think of the space between the "o" and the "f"

here    ✛

     of

as containing an infinite number of subdivisions within it. There's an infinity there. Take the space between the "o" and the "f" and halve it. Then halve that space. Then halve that space. And keep on going.[18] It's possible that the laws of physics place some limit on the ability to subdivide – that at some very small point, we reach a point of physical indivisibility – that an infinite division into something smaller and smaller and smaller ad infinitum is only mathematically conceivable in the abstract.

---

[18] Aquinas again: "That [differences of things] are infinite in number is revealed in two ways: in one way if we consider the multitude of differences in themselves; in another way if we consider the first genus as a first principle, for evidently innumerable differences are contained under it." AQUINAS, *supra*, note 13. See also René Descartes, Letter to Henry More (Feb. 5, 1649) in *Philosophical Letters* (Anthony Kenny, trans.) 242 ("God is the only thing I positively conceive as infinite."). Because no science can ever rest its intelligibility on an infinite number of qualities to subjects, a science which utilizes an infinite number of principles cannot exist. "For this reason, [Aristotle and Saint Thomas] thought that the existence of an Unmoved Mover, Uncaused Cause, was a necessary condition for the intelligibility of all science…" REDPATH, *supra* note 13, at 205. And, we might add, of all poetry.

If there is a very tiny unit which cannot be subdivided, then space is not infinitely divisible. The mountain climber would reach a point where it was physically impossible for him to make a smaller step than the last. The infinite in both directions may prove equally elusive. And in some sense, the finiteness of time imposes a kind of special limitation in any case; the mountain climber would have to stop making his tinier and tinier steps at the second coming when Christ descends from the clouds and says "Game over" even if the climber had not reached the tiniest possible step by then.

There is not an infinite number of atoms in the universe, just a (very) large number of atoms, to wit: between $10^{78}$ and $10^{82}$ atoms – that is, between ten quadrillion vigintillion and one-hundred thousand quadrillion vigintillion atoms. That is a lot. And some recent computations have suggested that the number might be $10^{86}$. That's an even bigger number – but a lot! But even *that* is a long way from an infinite number – $10^{\infty}$ atoms. An infinitely long way. Our universe has a finite mass.

Our universe is also finite in terms of its breadth (some 93 billion light years from end-to-end insofar as observations permit). There is only a certain amount of energy and mass in the universe. It seems that the majority of physicists today believe that the universe will continue expanding indefinitely or even for eternity given that there is not enough mass to reverse the expansion triggered by the big bang. Of course, it's tricky enough to weigh a parade of elephants or a crash of hippopotami, let alone the entire universe. The calculations might be revised someday and instead predict a universe which collapses back in on itself – presumably ending time in the same singularity which preceded the big bang. Of course, time might end in other scenarios, too, just as there are numerous scenarios in which Captain Kangaroo's hairstyle might become fashionable.[19]

Theology would predict that physics will also locate an endpoint in time; that time is finite on both ends since there is an end times which will greet us one morning. So far as we know, a division proceeding infinitely is possible, but I would not be terribly surprised if physics someday locates a point – a very, very small point – which cannot be subdivided. If an infinite division is unachievable in the material world (bound by limited matter, limited time, and limited divisibility), then we might conclude that infinity is merely conceptual in the material world. It only exists intellectually in this universe.

As Thomas Aquinas wrote, "if length were unlimited, a line would not exist, because a line is a measurable length (and this is why it is stated in the definition of a line that its extremities are two points)."[20] In the same way, dogma teaches that individuals have measured – mortal – lives in this world but enjoy the promise of immeasurable –

---

[19] See *supra* note 14.

[20] THOMAS AQUINAS, I COMMENTARY ON THE METAPHYSICS OF ARISTOTLE, Book 5, 1. 15, note 978.

immortal – life in the hereafter. Meditation on the infinite is a productive exercise and can, with the help of grace, help us to know God.

At any rate, an infinite opening-up in the middle of the second sentence of this work is what I'm trying to suggest: a blossoming; an unfolding of examples – an infinite or numberless expansion – something divine which we can sometimes glimpse indirectly. We know that we each have a finite number of breaths or heartbeats to enjoy, but imagining eternal life is more than just anticipating a reward or denying mortality, but something which participates in the divine, like – as *L*– taught – a person-for-person love participates in the divine. A bigness. An immensity; no –an Eternity. A footnote which goes and goes and goes… Is this something like little bit like God?

*   *   *

One emphasis here is that what *L*– begins with is a classification and division of things somewhat in the style of Aristotle. There are things. There are signs. There are a few subdivisions of each.

But – as his first sentence highlights, *L*–'s primary concern is with neither things nor signs but rather with doctrines; doctrines from which things and signs emerge; theological dogma, unity, and truth emerging somehow out of the chaos and multitude of matter; springing forth from the material world, its popular culture, its songs, its silliness, its tears, and its characters.

*  *  *

Finally, one brief sentence on the five magnificent pencil illustrations contained within the pages which follow: each was sketched by Yasemin Arkun from portions of surviving medieval illuminated manuscripts of *The Sentences*.

Thomas E. Simmons
Vermillion, South Dakota
June 2021

*Whew!*

*Do we get started <u>now</u>?*

*Or maybe take a short nap?*

1.

Every doctrine

springs

either
from a thing
or from a sign.

2.

Compared to –

*i*

Plutarch's halitosis –

which combed a mousehole
into his expert's commitments

burrowing for what seemed like
a timeless prison demarking their
increasing disinterest in one another

*ii*

A Green Giant's Moses

here

    now

        there

he stands, gloating awe, more than 200 meters high
poking his leafy temples above the flights of tern
with his fringed debt-goatee tugging to his chin

Shoulders reinforced with synthetics & carbon fiber
25 morals died in his construction; blown from his
brow after the 1st fiberglass chevalier toppled over

in 2110 during Cyclone Smith; Ringed with vines;
this arrogant colossus; Ridged by constellations
Fire-bush-beacon; our rune; our figure; our crest

What staggering fisc! Puckering a shadow outward
Maligning self-doubt: The Minnesota Canning Co.
in song: "Ho – ho – ho!" sliced expanding manna

across the veneer of Rice Lake; hands-on-hips
Lit at nighttime like Mount Rushmore only green
Buoyed; aqua; weight-lifting; high-handed (ha!)

"Ho – ho – ho!" ruffles expanding out – way out

past Austin – Grant adoración to our Shogun of the
Valley; our Dinty-Moore[21] of Faribault, legend has

it that his legs were fashioned from Doric columns
discarded from the local courthouse – Our Grassy
Supervisor, he is 'Progress' – he'll honor fibers &

Drunken Blue Earth cowers (one foot in a skin-like
Boot, the other untrod) Damn good merchandising!
Earlier tribes would've counted themselves blessed


*All right, all right; that was sobering.*

*No need to turn any more pages, OK?*

*Let's just <u>can</u> it*

*(ha!)*

---

[21] See *Thanks for the Memories*, ROSEMARY CLOONEY,
ROSEMARY CLOONEY SINGS BALLADS (Concord 1985) (side
A, track 1) (crooning: "Thanks for the memory / Of cushions
on the floor / Hash with Dinty Moore" etc. etc. etc.).

but these juried ones slumber until they "all rise /
Call the next case, bailiff…"

STATE OF KASHMIR     )
                             ss.
COUNTY OF USE      )

Petitioner –             )
A clump of crispy-    )     CIV. 09-173j
green-celery of a giant  )
                       )     COMPLAINT
vs.                   )
                       )
Respondent – Some jolly-  )
good-singing by Jack Ely –  )

*Listen, pal – t'ain't no fluke – I*

*I can't see goin'* ♪ *with a big-green*

*kook*[22]

Since no one wins in litigation, the case
resulted in a smashing verdict for Hormel
and the Jolly Green Giant™ just getting smashed

(ha!)

---

[22] *Jolly Green Giant*, THE KINGSMEN, VOLUME 3 (Jerden
Productions 1965) (side A, track 3).

A seashell splintered beneath a Holyoke cop's
      thumb[23]

Trying to break the resistance of an arsonist's
      will

Pointlessly (since a thumb can't break the chutzpah
      of

Ms. Madonna Ramadan Levy's new cotton twill
      wit

And Madonna Ramadan Levy couldn't give a rat's
      guild

For the life of some soapy goldfish collection) &
      yet

Accomplishing another gingery holy-sponge
      concession

Satiating our vinegary patrol's sobs o' delight @ the
      sight

Of her calamity housed in a cabinet I once
      constructed

Of stonemason Charles H. Pajeau's Tinkertoy™

---

[23] *Under my Thumb*, ROLLING STONES, AFTERMATH (Decca 1966) (side A, track 4).

kits

Though my teachers said it was 'a bit too Old
        Testament'

To fix anything above a *B-minus* yet giving me
        an

*A-minus* for worship with their damned free will
        report

Card-ing an underage dogmatism by layering in
        2

Cuss words she'll read into it, despite her foolish
        judge

Mint-barns and Mount Everest mini-steps past a
        lover; or

2, an honesty perforated with the same die she left
        me

4 seashells slivered with a starfish[24] ladder;
starship[25]
        chatter;

--------

[24] "We believe in fishermen, not dialecticians." PETER
LOMBARD, III THE SENTENCES 68 (Giulio Silano, trans.).

[25] Not to be confused with Jefferson Starship. Or with
Jefferson Airplane, for that matter. Or with THE JEFFERSONS
(1975-85) for *that* matter. And it does *matter*. See also *infra*
text accompanying note 94.

What at some point so in the far past passed for
        Bangla-
                desh

An apology to each and every Bangladeshi alive
        to-
                day

All one hundred and sixty-one million men and
        wo-
                men

I'm sorry ♪ I'm sorry ♪ I'm sorry ♪ I'm sorry ♪ I'm
sorry ♪ I'm sorry

I'm sorry ♪ I'm sorry ♪ I'm sorry ♪ I'm sorry ♪ I'm
sorry ♪ I'm sorry

I'm sorry ♪ I'm sorry ♪ I'm sorry ♪ I'm sorry ♪ I'm
sorry ♪ I'm sorry

etc.

*"One potato, two potato, three potato,
four"*

*"Stop right here; no need to do more"*

*v*

The all and the sundry

Winchesters with Solomon Grundy

A coyote & a roadrunner in Port-au-Prince

A cartoon bubble concerning time travel, since

after introducing my first-born to Doctor Who
and H.G. Wells at a too-tender age (always so
anxious, was I, to introduce him to what came
next that I often quoted a bumper sticker which
read: *Episode IV First: It's Just Good Parenting*)

I was a tad skeptical when he announced that he
had just finished constructing a time machine

Even more so as I saw he'd brought his blanket –
draped over an arm – as if it held a new utility

for him, though, pausing in whatever routine had
occupied me up to that moment, I mimicked at
him, lowering my pitch an octave, "Make it so"

Smoothly, he covered himself with his blanket,
sinking to the linoleum – the fabric collapsing
like a parachute in gym class — the air going out
of it until it took on his boy-shape, crouching

and I could see the rhythm of his apple-sized
lungs expanding and contracting like a pump

for 2 seconds

10

for three beats
for the 100<sup>th</sup> monkey …

Then he whipped off the blanket
and stood, erect and confident, the
demonstration seemingly complete

*Now*, he announced to the man
who was his father: *I'm in the future*

### ###

Saints Fabian & Sebastian     pray for us
Saints John & Paul            pray for us
Saints Cosmos & Damian        pray for us
Saints Gervase & Prostate     pray for us[26]

### ###

*Those worthy men: Tegghiaio, Farinata, Jacopo*
*Rusticucci, Arrigo, Mosca, the rest who set their*
*minds to merit well*[27] *– those men – writing*

**"Please don't turn the page"**

---

[26] *Graduale Romanum,* LITANIAE SANCTORUM 5 (1974).

[27] DANTE ALIGHIERI, DIVINE COMEDY (INFERNO), Canto 6
(Anthony Esolen, trans.).

oris f.ici
inies ven
leas me

*I see what you did there*


a man who wanted me to take care of myself / while drinking half a bottle of Wild Turkey® each night in a recliner that had seen / its better days / watching a Day-Day landing documentary / we had seen / better landings / and us both screaming / unplanned / in unison / "Get back in the *boats!*" / and fishing / day and night / staying in our own boat / his boat / a craft / a little river water in the bottom / mimicking river water in the riverbed / coax a few muskies / visit us / and remind us of a painting in the church[28] vestibule


Recall though, this sage – that on

*That day we did not read another page*[29]

---

[28] See *I'll Go to Church Again with Momma*, BUCK OWENS AND HIS BUCKAROOS, DUST ON MOTHER'S BIBLE (Capitol 1966) (side A, track 3).

[29] DANTE, *supra* note 27, Canto 5.

*vii*

Yeats' *Crucifixion*

*of an Outcast* decodes beatings; a diatribe
of vagabond-fish

The themes, of which, they say,

are intolerances; ficklenesses; A fisher
running afoul the monks

In London, Yeats

encountered his friend on the street; their speckled
wool nearly matched each others'

Conversation –

of Wilde's worries – or Yeats' essay – unmatched
their concerns for each other – but

Wilde <u>praised</u> *Outcast*:

'Sublime, wonderful, wonderful,'
Yeats' *Autobiography* would quote

Wilde's words, behind which

rooted Wilde's thorned legal trauma –
of what to <u>do</u> in the face of it –

Some'd suggested

14

that he: 'Inflate backyard balloons by hand,
so as to forge an escape' [sic]

    Gill-grasping notes

from Ireland, Wilde's face braided amity, as most
solids had urged him away; to bolt!

    but he'd declined …

Instead, he collapsed inwardly,
being slightly intoxicated

    Wilde's soul was not

ill-smelling. In Cork, he'd drawn fast the sad
demon of purgatory

    Paralysis

had gripped his wife but he never
rightly doubted just imprisonment

    Necessary

to give an account of the stuff – to go into
detail – it was not.

    Yeats could revamp

dank Londoners' commentary:
'Of infamy/new-Thermopylae'

Everyone knows

that cerebral meningitis would take Wilde
up in 1900

    'up, up, and away'[30]
    But before then

    'what goes up'[31] (…)
    A clock leaked –

    Yeat's eyes too –
    They dripped

    Still – before then:

two vexed beneficiaries could foresee kidney
ruptures in their kindness

    That day: the men

hugged on windy cobblestones – the gale caught
them off-guard

    They spun: the men

Far-off guards threatened Wilde's Irish words and
the puff

------

[30] Dionne Warwick, *Up, Up and Away*, DIONNE WARWICK IN VALLEY OF THE DOLLS (Scepter 1967) (side A, track 2).

[31] Sammy Davis Jr., *Spinning Wheel*, SOMETHING FOR EVERYONE (Motown 1970) (side A, track 1).

Pussed them too: the notes

all the 3<sup>rd</sup> words in them cycloned
ascended chaotically

  spinning[32] again 'Who was the monk?'

'Who were fish minstrels?' Wilde could wink, and
Yeats' reply cleaved in the breeze; it halted

  Neither could capture the letters back


*Wild*

*Still, let's give it a rest*

---

<sup>32</sup> See ibid.

*viii*

Trauma and autonomy in whatever flight
recorder you specify

And in whatever virtual quantities we fail to
count

There are plenty of poems which make
various quiddities of the same sherbert-tinted

things
their centerpiece

living alone; the back-and-forth sweep
of ovation signs splicing uncooked lamb

their distressed
naif-NASA veins; their jars

their shutter falls[33]
reject a surreal pastiche

their nourished bruises
lawless skulls

which need not be replicated
here unless you beg

---

[33] *Peg*, STEELY DAN, AJA (ABC 1977) (side B, track 1).

for it / for an atom / <u>each</u> atom belonging to me / and
to you / blood atoms / creeds whether in abeyance or
not / soil atoms / ant atoms / schools too / the air that
Walt was in love with in his mouth / haughtiness and

tobacco salt squashing it all / up

Inches of organs / all which inches

His life in the ward, his early life

That which wags / the wages of men

bracing sex / An elaborate identity

"The procreant urge of the world"

Hugging bedfellows / some bitter

The origins of poems he barricaded

and delivered, and died of

*x*

the sum of 'em

the earth-body with all its critters strapped thereto
the lakes and mantles, the junk, and the musk-oxen

the cinema we make of all of that
plastic toys and a maroon libretto

spelunkers and parched parachutes
heraldry and croisers  the uniformed
                          the uninformed

The River Named      Po
The One Telly Tubby *Not* Named Po

fond and wayward tinky-winky stubby-
thoughts; my mother's font of thinking

your artifacts          their archeology
a crusty character      ready for grilling
a crust of coal-pipe    ripe for drilling

a crumpling burl        a den of thieves

Dr. Zhivago             Hotter Chicago

her material culture    our immaterial biases

    questions which everyone
    has asked such as –

20

'Has Slim Whitman *really* sold more records in
Europe than the Beatles?'

'Is Zamfir really the *master* of the pan flute?

'Why did the soldier offer Jesus *vinegar*?'

'Is Bobby Flay *that* hard to beat?'

> things which *no one has ever thought*
> *to ask* and no one ever will ask such as –

'Why are there so preciously few poems about toilet
training?'

A Frankenstein beaver-creature which doesn't give
a dam to the Bay of Pigs flood relief program; who
doesn't even pretend to try indefensible malpractice
cases to a jury; who hasn't been around much lately

The Golden Girls       Faust
Uncle Quah's Coffee  House

everything limp and   docile and extrinsic
the G*damn Federal   Sentencing Guidelines

the Avengers movies  legalized marijuana

chemical equations    abortion clinics
sunny domes           caves of ice

everything firm and   active and intrinsic

21

the Six Day War
the Ikea® catalog
[front-to-back]
Susan Sontag
[back-and-front]
robust rose hips
which don't lie
Basil Gogos
[front-and-center]
Monte Cassino


cyclic vomiting        syndrome diagnoses
obstreperous Yiddish boombox melodies


The Ministry[34]       of Gregor Mendel
How he fell            for him [M. Ali]
was *he*               Sonny Liston?


& what a piss-
tun! + ta-da!
"*x*" / "double you"
ex-why ze-bra!?
the "y" in "because we like you" [Mickey M.]
one "hee-hee" to three
Hee-Haw episodes
the trolley narrow-gauge


in the land of        make-believe
Gerald Vizenor this   cream-crushed ore


don't be frightened   of this, Hezbollah
haven't you ever      seen a phylum before

---

[34] See MINNISTRY, WITH SYMPATHY (Arista 1982).

Even Siddharta
Figs in Jakarta
Your f_**king
f_**king        Magna Carta[35]

Patterson's tower her  underground dower
Kaveripoompattinam  during rush hour

Its street-stall dumplings
steaming long after dark
its orthodox stretch marks
its Pollyanna politics
its Iggy Pops

its                     sketchy
brownie                 mixes

three-out-of-four       dentists of
the apocalypse          recommend
tridents for            their patients
who stab                deforestation
dragons habituated      to devouring
Parisian women          of ill repute
wearing pinstripes      on suits of
breadfruit-taproot      commutes
to Beirut in hot        pursuit of
all these things        and what else?[36]

---

[35] Magna Carta Libertatum (1215-).

[36] See *passim* (re: sympathetic readings between the lines,
a/k/a sympathetic strings (of lines)). Not to be confused with
string theory. But see also the little samba number titled
*Sympathy for the Devil*, THE ROLLING STONES BEGGARS
BANQUET (Decca 1968) (side A, track 1).

Well Grief ≈ for One

When a kid falls in it

and Lassie doesn't give a

roster; she just mocks her

A tv dinner ≈ for U

Hungry Man™ Tunneled

covered over; logging

but boring deeper

making polka-dots

and not healing

any

Time soon[37]

---

[37] *Time in a Bottle*, JIM CROCE, YOU DON'T MESS AROUND WITH JIM (ABC 1972) (side B, track 3).

25

toilet training                    *mutatis mutandis*

toilet training                    *ceteris paribus*

happy?

**With the incessant page turning?**

**No, not exactly – No, No, I'm <u>not</u> happy**

*xiii*

when at long

long last she
fingered out
the last round
turnip from the
cooling ground
parceled all the
nutmeg and un-
loosed the hang
nail man's noose
from the rubber band[38]
and finally emphasized
that autonomy of which she'd
dreamed in a cot made of social
media pamphlets and only then realized
her legal rights to cancel *Sports Illustrated*

Baal was not her favored next step
but she took to it anyway like a
rooting tooting cowboy gal as
found in her strongly favored
Atlanta Falcons® patterned
curtains keeping out the
lava & not caring how

her late husband used
to knot them up with
his corn-festered
feet and ask for

---

[38] THE BAND, MUSIC FROM BIG PINK (Capitol 1968).

26

the first mug of
coffee before
she'd even
extricated
herself
from her
O'Keefe
bed; called
out for
'Fred'
The
sky
was
liberal
when
his
head –
they
found
dead –
among
her
they
said –
along with
her dread-locks ferns
among her pervert David Byrne among
1,000,000,000,000 women & children & divorces to
find

Tardigrades earning and enjoying their natures
in hot springs / deep seas / shingles on my roof

Terrestrial tardigrades adhering to liverworts
and feeling most comfortable with a water film

And some have articulated in space
Some have unravelled on the moon
Released haphazardly in the lunar dust

like a bin-full of spider-babies[39]

They're 'dead' there of course
But a well-aimed
droplet from a dropper
might well reanimate them
yawning as they awoke adorably

like unborn kittens[40]
It's not that any extreme environment
is their briar patch

They're extremophilic
Still, they don't even

bother to growl
at gamma-ray bursts

---

[39] See SPIDER BABY (American General Pictures 1967).

[40] Meowing, *e.g.*, "mew, mew, mew, mew, ♪" etc.

or large meteorite impacts
They take them in their

not-quite-microscopic
bear-like gait-strides

They take them in stride
They take them in concert[41]

with their uniform habits;
their multifarious habits

High dosages of radiation
are to these ones

almost as refreshing
as fresh green tea balls
of silver mesh

which will possess          mailing bean spurts

Nature turning itself treacly   Nature turning dour

The morbid & the rock star   Silken flesh

---

[41] THE DOORS, IN CONCERT (Elektra 1970).

*xv*

'Gilgamesh'

– not the kind of name a boy sets his designs

    on for glory if he wants to avoid getting
    socked in the gut on the playground every

Recess

    which ages the playground participants more
    than their underpaid adult supervisors[42] googling

Blake Shelton

    as contemptible as any celebrity i never knew

Averroes 'the Commentator' (a/k/a Ibn Rushd)

    who never knew

Sally Field sainted in 'The Flying Nun' (1967-70)

    and so pretty it pained me to watch her

    as an 8-year-old elf leaning
    into a 19-inch-screen[43]

---

[42] Ray Bradbury, *The Playground*, ESQUIRE 28 (Oct. 1953).

[43] Manufactured by Setchell Carlson.

*xvi*

*

* Saint *
* Agnes *
*


men would besiege her as if she were castles
She'd palm mortar to each new leak with a

pueblo's
carapace

But a gun advanced to put words in her fortifications

before he left her taking a 'plan *B*' pill she didn't
want for any sleep-for-days sting-rayed admission

curling
up

in an almost-sail-baby's estuary, fetal-style –

nails puncturing the finger sounds of feral wire
Carnages claim their verse-chains as much as her

seines set
flowery rosary floats

Push chitin layers in there, deep; deep tissue

pushed she pushed him back deeply with an oar's
arc connecting; collating animal heads two-by-

two
Her backbone

down-welled the punctuation his words mouthed

rough Words; as one mouth dredged up a water-
furrow waving "*am*" – it was circled / it circled her

circular sheepskin
scroll-like wagons

circle them against arrows and ought to swipe-delete

coral-ghost    condensations:    a    'teach-u-to-fish'
scribbled here caged Chopin to-be-trawled *in* by an

epipelagic woman's arrows
like this one

Three syllables down; creaking tabernacle timbers

A ropey ladder and thick sets of gillnets collapsing
Flanking the littoral, on her garrison, fast; a stalking

of mind
muffled

inside the shoal's current; unfurled; burned. Hoist

decoupled chroma to toughen their ballast-tank joints
Lightning spews some rough lumber-thunder voiced

An *"I"*
Deliberates

A *"You"*
Conjugates

toward a chatter-marked breach. She'll foist buckets

of letters into her mouth, the new anchor felt sublime
As ballads beat it back to sea, dying for the tawny

climb her back
shone

sweat-beads from that woman-rowing-time

###

Get on the Ark ♪ Get on the Ark ♪ Get on the Ark ♪
Get on the Ark ♪ Get on the Ark ♪ Get on the Ark ♪

###

Row, row, row

###

"Get on the bus"          "Forget about us"[44]

*Forget about turning pages!*

---

[44] Tony Orlando and Dawn, *Tie a Yellow Ribbon Round the Ole Oak Tree* (Bell 1973) (single)

34

## *You failed to forget*

4 in a row on *Jeopardy* in which the answer read by the late great Alex Trebek under the subject heading "Old Testament" (for $300) is –

> "Nicknamed 'the Troubler of Israel'"

And the correct question is:

> "Who is Elijah?"

And where the contestant – who claims to be a housewife from Finger, Tennessee[45] – misses the next four-hundred-dollar question under the same heading by responding (correctly),

> "Who is Elijah's father?"

---

[45] The birthplace of Buford Hayse Pusser (1937-1974), Sheriff of McNairy County, Tennessee, credited with surviving seven stabs and eight shots, before his fiberglass hot rod Corvette crashed and burned with him outside of it (ejected like a hard plastic cassette tape) just after he'd signed a contract with Bing Crosby's company. See *Buford Pusser's Walkin' Tall*, EDDIE BOND, SINGS THE LEGEND OF BUFORD PUSSER (Enterprise 1973) (side A, track 2); *The Buford Stick*, DRIVE-BY TRUCKERS, THE DIRTY SOUTH (New West 2004) (side B, track 2).

to the answer, which had first been dutifully read by that dapper Canadian host with perfect teeth was,

"Sobach[46]"

And the daily-double answer (accompanied by appropriate daily-double jinglings) was,

"What Sobach saw at Elijah's birth"

To which the correct question (for a generous $900) was,

"What are sixteen angels
feeding Sobach's baby
orange crinkle-flames,
spooning them into
that cherub-mouth,
and swaddling him in
blue-tipped licking fire
in the third season of
*Torched by an Angel*?"[47]

---

[46] The producers were also prepared to accept "Solomon Zalman Kremer" (1695-1758) who was the father of Vilna Gaon (a/k/a Elijah ben Solomon Zalman, a/k/a HaGaon Rabbenu Eliyahu) (1720-97).

[47] An apology to each and every man named after Michael Landon alive today; all one hundred and sixty-one of them:

I'm sorry ♪ I'm sorry ♪ I'm sorry ♪
I'm sorry ♪ I'm sorry ♪ I'm sorry ♪

resulting in perfectly-timed applause from the polite,
well-behaved, and largely Caucasian studio audience
which predictably swallows up large-scale forest-fire

skies-drenched

<hr>

I'm sorry ♪ I'm sorry ♪ I'm sorry ♪
I'm sorry ♪ I'm sorry ♪ I'm sorry ♪
I'm sorry ♪ I'm sorry ♪ I'm sorry ♪
I'm sorry ♪ I'm sorry ♪ I'm sorry ♪
I'm sorry ♪ I'm sorry ♪ I'm sorry ♪ etc.

*xviii*

lies

french-

fries quench-dyes waving "bye-bye" the last time[48]

– "not I –
not @ 1st"

sighs I not

something I ever expected to relish, coming as it
did from a child I barely agreed to babysit for $3
CAD in October of 1973 – and when I did,
erupting into a dialectical inauguration which
lasted into my late teens, cross-word puzzling a
list of all former boyfriends, some of them down,
some across, and three outliers who managed a
diagonal-ity, the one named 大畠 (which "might"
mean "large glory" according to the website
www.20000-names.com – making it sound a little
bit profane) & who is especially difficult to match
with Betzalel (which means "shadow of God"
according to www.aish.com – making it sound
kind of holy) where they intersect each other, the
kanji getting into a switchblade fight with the
Roman letters in a rainswept, roped-off area,

---

[48] *Bye Bye Love*, THE EVERLY BROTHERS (Cadence 1958)
(side A, track 3).

The big bang,

A child I killed,

The one I married,

A 2<sup>nd</sup> so-called 'friend'

whose name I've forgotten,

Paul, my *1ˢᵗ* friend, Saint Paul and his Doctor Luke
who had a talent for Christology as well as for slap-
stick routines – as with the case of Eutychus – a
teen from Troas tended by Paul as Paul

(as Paul was sometimes wont to)

droned like a drone on-and-on-and-on-and-on
sending his homily like little paper airplanes (before
they were invented) over the crowd as night fell

as Eutychus listened from his 3ʳᵈ-story Roman
window and as he got

sleepier and sleepier he nodded and fell *ker-plop* out
of the window like an egg, end-over-end-over-end-
over-end onto the street – dying

but Paul revived him

Eutychus was fortunate and Eutychus *means*
fortunate and fortunate he was[49]

My other friends Saint Augustine – Jean on the run

Saint Margaret Mary Alacoque – 2ⁿᵈ to none

'Ol Father David – having his fun

---

[49] *Acts* 20:7-12.

*xx*

2<sup>nd</sup> from the sun

pilgrims ignore her – except for / her too-rare
transits

& her phases – this 2-bright grubby / brown-bland
sphere

oppressed within folds / of a mono-chromatic
samite

as shapeless as she's formulaic / orbiting a thin
banana-slice

turned cosmos-edgewise / & so much hotter than
us

thus pocked with many marks this / low pocketless
gentle-woman

and snaffled of even / a single gibbous wafer
she's

as self-absorbed as an oyster / those trojan asteroids
holding

their pace; skating her tapestries count / not as her
moons; those

dwellers in a dark-verge / enjoying bits
of

*xxi*

it

that
*exspiro*
i mean u

pagan poets u

all urge the flimsiness of spirits
All whispy, translucent, weaklings
Now-you-see-them-now-you-don't
Apparitions with a macabre facet

Not so – they're tough little jobs
Here's a simile:
Spirits are like rivets so
Don't drop one on your boot[50]

Invoke the fist-sized rivets
Tying the hull of the Titanic together
Granted they're what failed her
Some Irish welder not minding his task

But I've seen images of her
Some ten leagues down
And in large measure
They're still holding fast
Still skating *her* tapestry

---

[50] *These Boots Were Made for Walkin'*, NANCY SINATRA
(Reprise 1965) (single).

And here's a proof:
A bearded monk shot and beaten
Whipped and shot a few more times
Then tossed into an icy river: *Sploosh!*

*His* still held taut for quite a spell
Before his body – all crumpled
Soft, corruptible – gave it up and
Even then it was barely winded

Took flight over Moscow it did
Yelping like a cowgirl set free[51]
The spirit is seated in there pretty good
It's wedged in there awful tight

And when one does pop loose

Look

out –

---

[51] See *Rasputin*, BONEY M., NIGHTFLIGHT TO VENUS (Atlantic 1978) (side A, track 2).

below!

for food, and for cafeteria food-fights, as journeys

require propellants, one sort or another – peppered
meats for mountain hikes up bark-covered paths
Barber chairs and penny farthings
Cigarettes rolled for priests
Wood matches for rockets
Search-notes for gospels
A full teat for a babe
Ash for cinders
Bras for teens
Casting 4 us
Commands
Sanctity
Liturgy
Desire
Water
Bread[52]
Spirit
Wine
Dust
God
One
We
!

---

[52] *Don't Shut Me Out*, BREAD (Elektra 1969) (side B, track 2).

made crank calls such as the ones Jerry Lewis
made and released on a vinyl lp for $6.95 +
state and local sales tax[53]

A two-tone Dorothy Lynch dressage whistle
made of buffalo horn featuring a triller with a
cork pea complete with a braided non-adjust-
able neck-cord

Unlicensed Montessori day care centers outside
of Tupelo, Missouri

Apologies people don't make before they die

Everything ever written in Coptic or Sanskrit

Apologetics in the margins of sheet music

A mess of misguided drywall projects

Mrs. Robinson's real name

Misunderstood gaps

Sage bundles

Jackalopes

---

[53] JERRY LEWIS, PHONEY PHONE CALLS 1959-1972 (Sin-
Drome Records 2001).

MeWe

Donuts

Grass

Myth

Lead

Laps

Bins[54]

Ruts

Ham

Die[55]

Sod[56]

Us

&

---

[54] *Bin Laden*, IMMORTAL TECHNIQUE, MOS DEF, AND DJ GREEN LANTERN (Babygrande Records 2005) (single).

[55] *Live and Let Die*, WINGS, WINGS GREATEST (Capitol 1978) (side A, track 3).

[56] *Green Green Grass of Home*, JERRY LEE LEWIS, COUNTRY SONGS FOR CITY FOLKS (Smash 1965) (side A, track 1).

All the rest of history, by way of example:

Back before bishops wore mitres like rockets
There was a knocking – the pope was knocking
When the servant heard it, she approached the door

She heard his voice / recognized it / knew him/ who
it was / It was Simon Peter / Joyous & forgetting
to open the door, she rushed back to tell
the others, and announced: "It's Peter!"

"It's Peter!" Meanwhile,
the pope kept on knocking
– somewhat more irritably knocking –
while the assembled guests in John Mark's
mother's parlor waved the servant girl away
"You're out of your mind," mumbled one of them

She persisted: "It's him." They ignored her more
"Well, then it must his *angel*," they guffawed
They thought he was a ghost / while *he*
thought he was a dream / The pope
thought the whole affair dreamt
-up but still he kept on knock-
ing / & Rhoda? / Tenacious
Rhoda was within her
ecclesial authority
to manage
doorway[57]
jokes

---

[57] *Acts* 12:12-15.

including knock-knock ones

and the rest of future history

and

The same birthmark as Shirley Temple broasted in a

> hurricane lamp, her hand in mine as we
> weighed the flamboyance of celebrity
> impermanence on a beach before she turned
> 9 with no idea *then* how long movie fans
> would pin her posters

The oil-sheen likened to a collection of slave cases in

> which is discussed how a security interest can
> be perfected in a chattels real, which is just
> another name for human beings, who were at
> once both movable (and hence *chattels*, from
> the Norman French word for cattle) and semi-
> permanently attached to the land like a fence
> post (and hence *real*; signifying realty) sunk
> into dirt up to the line

Several French televisions repossessed by assignors

> and successors-in-interest to the pay-day-
> lender-creditors of varied living descendants
> of Shirley Temple's ancestors and slaves of
> the Newland home where my sister still lives
> in a mobile home

> in

Mobile, Alabama[58]

The beautiful men living there who are relatively

> lowbred at competitive free-floating
> logrolling despite their very best intentions
> and endless after-school practices which
> leave them spent and limp and widespread

*versus*

---

[58] *Sweet Home Alabama*, LYNYRD SKYNYRD, SECOND HELPING (MCA 1974) (side A, track 1).

beautiful immobile men *skilled* at competitive free-
floating logrolling

typical defendants buttoned-up and flannel-clad
although neither is required by either the United
States Log Rolling Association (USLRA) or the
Canadian Logger Sports Association (CAN-LOG)
(ha!)

with their various techniques

sharing the log with their rival

with water too-iced for swimming

as their playing field and simultaneously their judge

and let's not forget the 'Lumber Jills' like Jenny
Atkinson – born in Grand Marais on the North
Shore, who earned her master's from Saint Mary's,
teaches schoolchildren in Stillwater, competed right
through her breast

cancer, a three-time champion in both logrolling
and *boom running* –

whose determined mouth is all you need to know
about your chances; a circle ratio which takes into
account

the precise number of bog bodies in Lake Superior
secreted in the pagan pockets of underwater ravens
manifesting a sort of … a sort of prude clowder of

brutes swimming at all the wrong

        angles

projecting, "we too were like arrows in our

        own hands

a horn will sprout" and diving into menacing seed

at right        angels

to one an        other[59]

enclosed within taverns lacking an immense exit
lacking more than that which even Gordon Light
Foot[60] could sing of within her tombstone grooves

        deep down in the continuous
        Some things hiding
        and hidden, well-
        paraphrased, but
        hidden as owls
        hiding from sight

---

[59] Pope Gregory: *Non Angli sed angeli.*

[60] (b. 1938) (not the autoboot character from *Transformers*).

all these misguided trilobite reviews:

*Maybell Q.* ***½

    IMO the best for the money
    Your gunna luv em honey
    Seen others not as hairy

    Others with red eyes
    Not nearly as realistic
    A bit?

    small I'd buy them again
    Shipping slow
    for my taste

*An Amorous Customer* ****

    We set a dozen up in my folks'
    Steinway Baby Grand & then

    hid in the quartzite fireplace
    to observe
    their surprise

    Marvelous!!!!!!!
    unmatched joys!
    Soft too Huge!!!

*Sir Faithful Jonathan Edwards Fortescue* **

    If you use a bone-stock

these dissolve
almost immediately

unless you fold in oyster crackers
a commercial grade stool softener
or poach them

first Chef K has a post
on it <u>here</u> <link deleted>

*anon.* ***

Disappointed
These travel far better than the
pom-pom creatures

we'd tried
earlier
but ours
were lost

They were an anniversary gift
from our son
before we
misplaced
him too

*Iran* *½

Our twins
selected this as a science project

They
followed the instructions

but our kit lacked a queen

The water
went sour

Their teacher
gave them all *D*'s

The worker-trilos
ate each others'

planets they'll sever prophets

They'll never
be the same

*BlueJ* *

Not for beginners
to commodity trading
especially if you expect
a TRILOBITE!!!!!!!!!!!!!!!!!!!!!!!!!!!!!!!!!!!!!!

I did not receive
a TRILOBITE ! ! ! ! !
& so had to
resort to lychee
nut futures
on margin !
otherwise 5 stars

## Are you <u>still</u> turning pages?


the way that an Israeli space agency manages
to spill Tardigrades all over the moon no-no
no, I am not making this up ask Rhoda or
Alexa or the World Book Encyclopedia set

salesman you always wanted to screw and
confirmation will snap its nerf-ball jaws on
to your doubt like fog on the masts of a ghost
ship plowing through tired, groggy metaphors

parting them open to reveal memoried vistas of

*xxx*

Deuel County, South Dakota flocks

    flapping, spring-embodied
    pressed to sodden, tawny fields

    spangled among reeds
    still more pierced within the air

    sprayed against cloud cover like spilled opiates

    multitudes of them sluicing northward
    those numberless pilgrims numberless

    and to say they are honking
    would be as if to say that
    a church choir is guffawing

    rather they (the fleshy-feathered; the pink-
    footed)

    they proclaim the transcendent and they wonder
    at it, their throats frosted, promised, astonished,
    then stilled by

    the vault

    wherein they surge

57

right smack-dab into Allahabad, India's
bright-green cement roadside brontosauri

    six

    of

    'em

    autumn-quieted
    pointlessly oriented; numbered
    Wonderfully rounded in the curling tail segments

    like Play-Doh®

    *pooft*!

The stacking of French toast
with way too much syrup

    sun-buttered
    cinematically soaked
    oligarchs – chemically a robust gasp-slant

    illustrated for the pre-K crowd

    *delicious*!

The French toast – *not* the pre-K crowd for
heaven's sake – for heaven's gate # four steering
clear don't swerve –

hug the center line down-shifting a word

keep it in the lines!

(the color-book lines)

hold the line!

(the phone line)

what's my line?!

(we don't know)

what's this line ⁺ for?

it's a Muncie 4-speed down-

shifting and crossing a fine-line

(just absurd – William Byrd;

his notes of curd) let's not say 'turd'

until the third

*Now <u>this</u> would be a good place*

*for a bookmark*

## ...*or not*

inning flattening the curve
a longing for decrees
the draining of bees
the cashew nuts in a
thousand and one
tonsil recipes my
forehead my warhead
my late father
my elderly mom
a rusty pimple
a hermit-crab
a pocket-tab
the magi the monsoon
the discarded
MAGA hats
the thin mints
the thick-men bum-
rushing the capital
breaking a pane
barging butane
killing cops
the way that
Kipling could
turn a phrase
the way that
pepper spray
can turn you
off too

*xxxiii*

both horse and rider like stubble


the blast of nostrils

the water piled up

dividing the spoils


the inhabitants of Philistia

the chiefs of Edom

inside a snowglobe


atop Shuri bitterness

the friend from work
who would stop by

unannounced when
ever i signaled she
shouldn't

blasting an array
of wet bathtub
woodworking projects

denting her '96
Proton Tiara's
structural rigidity

collapsing what
had taken all day to inflate

each time she
miscalculated the Dresden

blue driveway and clipped
my timidity

with her carelessness
despite how much
I enjoyed her

warriors[61]

her polo buttons

her scripture quotes

her dimples – all just too morose

her latest Covid booster-dose

her

Julio Iglesias – *adios*

her Walter Mercado – *grandiose*


*if you keep on turning pages*

*you might begin to turn toward*

*something else*

---

[61] *Gonna Fly Now (Theme Song from* Rocky*)*, ROCKY: ORIGINAL MOTION PICTURE SCORE (United Artists Records 1976) (side A, track 1); see also *The Warrior*, SCANDAL, FEATURING PATTY SMYTH, THE WARRIOR (Columbia 1984) (side A, track 1).

The authentic champion in *Shogun Warriors*:

When Michael Casey, a Cistercian religious of
Tarrawarra, spoke of the attitude expressed by

monastic clothing, and explained that it ought to be
*the sort of clothes no respected denizen of the*
*worldly city would ever want to be seen wearing*

And as Ilongo Savage[62] – an oceanographer of
Madagascar – puts on the 900-ton Planetary Robot

Dangard Ace suit, he does so *like anyone else*, yet
adds – genially – *that is, one leg at a time* – winking
and veneering a cloak of ersatz-modesty robed-ink

Ilongo Savage defines a well-groomed and pectoral-
defined example of a respected denizen of a worldly

city, hastily pulling on his pants *two legs at once*,
while the unarmed Judith Johns distracts the grotto
thing 'Starchild' just long enough for Savage to

finish zipping, buckling. and tucking himself in
No one would ever mistake Ilongo Savage for an

ascetic and no one would confuse a Shogun Warrior

---

[62] Not to be confused with Doc Savage (a/k/a Clark Savage,
Jr.). More pelagic than Blake Lively in *The Shallows*. See THE
SHALLOWS (Columbia Pictures 2016).

with a die-cast toy armed with a spring-loaded
sharpened *shuriken* & licensed by Mattel® from the

creators of the garish *tokusatsu* television programs
Still, Ilongo Savage fights the same daily interior /

exterior battles on *more than one plane at once* as
his sensei would observe after battling 'Starchild,'
Savage is made a prisoner like St. Paul on the moon

and detonates his power packs in an attempt to win
and when 'the Thing' 'in the Grotto[63]' blinks at

Savage, its fangs close *snap!* with its single eyeball-
tentacle-tongues spouting from its monocular
eyelashes – it's all uni-eye and teeth and tentacles –

it's an eye mounted on a celery stalk; the most
horrible of Dr. Demonicus' many, many monsters

Later, re-suited, battle boots humming, o're craig
and fen flies Savage again trying to outflank
'Starchild' but he is tank-sided by a tentacle and

twin boot-blasts blind the demon's mono-pupil for
an instant's reprieve and in the primary color palate,

---

[63] Not to be confused with Ben Grimm from the Fantastic
Four. More tragic than Daniel Day-Lewis (and no relation to
Jerry Lewis) as the voice actor for Deputy Dawg. See DEPUTY
DAWG: THE MOVIE (United Artists 1981) (unmade); *supra*
note 53 (citing Jerry Lewis (a/k/a Joseph Levitch)). No
relation to Jerry Lee Lewis (a/k/a 'The Killer'), either. *Supra*
note 56.

faint vespers of spiritual warfare can be discerned
Scuba-diving scientist Judith Jones is *unarmed* but
*lovely-armed* and the story's center she rests

comfortably in her stiff courage as her lungs aerate
from her air cylinders, but her heart lacks enough
$O_2$ to tell that garishly painted, well-panted Savage
exactly how she feels about him; what she wants of
in this narrative of *Shogun Warriors*; there was no

elephant-in-the-room but there was a prudent monk-
in-the-room, and her name was Dr. Jones – only she

had the strength and inward justice to fire her fists
at the chaos-causer – only she could hold aloft
'Starchild' by recalling a humility of her own steel[64]

---

[64] Not to be confused. Not to be confused. Not to be confused.
See HORATIO ALGER, RAGGED DICK AND OTHER CHANTS FOR
SUCCESSFUL BRONCHITIS PROFITMAKING (1890).

exorcising a handful of ammonite auto-engines[65]

& some of their internet pica-font listings

| | |
|---|---|
| *'62* | Ad says: "Ran when parked" |
| *Avanti* | "Never got around to it" |
| | "Wife making me sell" |

| | |
|---|---|
| *'82* | One piston wheezes |
| *Camaro* | Cheaper plastic can't be found |
| | The air con worked well |

| | |
|---|---|
| *'23* | Assembly *"required"*?! |
| *Mercedes* | Not entirely accurate – |
| *VW Kit Car* | In truth, *optional* |

| | |
|---|---|
| *3.0 Straight* | I wish to engage |
| *Six* | with an engine with which I |
| | share integrity |

| | |
|---|---|
| *'68* | Capped messenger god |
| *Cougar* | It's its grill that steals our coins |
| | Haunting G-man's rest |

| | |
|---|---|
| *'22* | Uniflow engine |
| *Doble* | the root of all problems – yet |
| *Model D* | Joy's valve gear retained |

| | |
|---|---|
| *2000* | Crazy low mileage |

---

[65] *Cars*, GARY NUMAN, THE PLEASURE PRINCIPLE (Beggars Banquet 1979) (side B, track 4).

| | |
|---|---|
| *Boxster* | a missing gas cap; trailered<br>Stolen license plates |
| *2002*<br>*Proton*<br>*Arena* | We ridiculed her<br>without mercy about it<br>… but it had promise |
| *'66*<br>*IH*<br>*Scout* | The American<br>flag took up the greater part<br>of the driver's door |
| *'34*<br>*Fords* | She gushed about them<br>in her poured-into dress of<br>cartoon characters |
| *2021*<br>*Mahindra*<br>*Thar* | Strong Greek variant<br>Too rich for my blood by half<br>MPG? Don't ask! |
| *'66*<br>*Beetle* | I spray painted it<br>in a carwash parking lot:<br>Black over sky tones |
| *'79*<br>*Renault*<br>*LeCar* | French joker! Stripped off<br>half the twin-panel-sticker<br>Now it just reads: 'Car' |
| *'63*<br>*Thunderbird* | Cost me six hundred<br>Our Fathers to get across<br>South Dakota's breadth |

xxxvii

to see the opening act

center-parting the curtain for the next show –

Please welcome… Chaoskamph! [applause]

*Chaos's just a Hebrew word for*
*Tohu Wa-bohu*, an alternative
reality Janis Jop[66] scratched into a tin

Shure microphone, gripping its stem
like a sign reading *Repent the End*
*is Near*, when in fact the end wasn't

within spitting distance of Alcatraz
whose scratchy throated walls could
almost be discerned in the dampened

diesel from all that spit-depth
charging the tents, out in the Bay
where a something hovered over it

just over the surface of accents
deep enough for the sound guy
to wire quantum garden sockets

*In the beginning, plod-inflated some*
*leavens and the mirth*, crooned her

---

[66] *Me and Bobby McGee*, JANIS JOPLIN, PEARL (Columbia
1971) (side B, track 2).

3 alternative-reality abyss-crooners
'Fu and the gang' they called themselves

~~Fu breached; forever abdicated~~

who preached but never levitated
at least until - *pow*! - their nightly show
crashed since ticket tricks profited them a lot

fought them distraught
not a slop-cot
brought when
/ sought a lie-grin / caught my foreskin / un-knot-
ted swirl-slop  Get His phone .    fizz-nit
                t-His poem isn't finished

~~The blueprints aren't thongs~~
~~Doc's wetsuit was bronzed~~
~~She'd crushed on the Fonz~~

no! for God's sake don't
stir it anymore        stop

u can't cook some
thing defectively if

no One has even got out
the f**king ingredients yet

pause two beats // wait for it

*So, wait for it*

*Nicely*

*Why*
*Don't*

*You*

## *nicely done*

you turned the page you tried
and true methodology
for burying a horse, you, to wit


### 

When your daughter's
horse dies, don't bury it

right away – hold-off on
the back-hoe – leave it

on the prairie to attract the coyotes –

wait a spell – then settle in to pick

them off with a small
caliber rifle refine-scoped
from a reasonable distance
as this is a sensible thing to do
It's just ranching as we know it

Or rather, it's just ranching & we know it

Still, neither of us parents are insensitive

to our daughter's anxious pitch –
her teen-puckers and scowls –
as she turns up the bathroom
faucet to overcome the

click-relay of polished
cantered shots while
readying a contact
lens on her index
finger before
pivoting &
aiming
it

When your daughter's
horse dies, hold-off on

the back-hoe – but not
for long for
unnamed horses rot[67]

                    ###

you finished
this one
but you sure
gave me fits    o!                                        try

                                     another dripping?

---

[67] *A Horse with No Name*, AMERICA (Warner Bros. 1972) (side
A, track 5).

75

try this, drip-drop:

"qti32sw4edroof6t7u980i-opkijlhubgvcf7tg6y)(x#"

try all of the different ways of typing this ↑ line

all of its different variations

including all gibberish and those which amount to
each and every saline-soaked line of *Pierre: or, the
Ambiguities*, Hamsun's *Pan*, Gorky's *Childhood*,
the Torah, *The Tao of Pooh*, the Heinlein juveniles,
*Setting Free the Bears*, and all the rudimentary-
grade tourist-trade elementary school union-
negotiated muddy-ape-lines I'm typing now, etc.

| every tick | every tock |
|---|---|
| all types | of bears |
| go there | and figure |

I'll wait while we consider –

1. a good faith count of the atoms in the universe[68] –

$$300,000,000,000,000,000,000,000,000,000,0$$
$$00,000,000,000,000,000,000,000,000,00$$
$$0,00,000,00,000,000,000$$

---

[68] GEORGE GAMOW, ONE TWO THREE ... INFINITY: FACTS AND
SPECULATIONS OF SCIENCE 16-18 (1953).

2. each atom containing a very tiny printing press generating random lines of text made up of the 26 letters, the ten figures 0-9, and 14 common signs

like $ and * and ( and @

and so on

thereby generating (mostly) lines such as this ⁺
"qti32sw4edrOof6t7u980i-opKijlhUbgcf7tg6y)(x#"

but occasionally such as this ⁺
"Foreign@might'super@ClassicFrontalpic/KLear"

and – eventually – even like this one⁺
"chock-full of clever phrases, she said, kittenishly"[69]

and this one ⁺
"gun-wads and axle-grease, fat country 'tis Arras"[70]

and this one ⁺
"Mine is longer by three feet of steel, yes, yes"[71]

and so on

3. each atom's printing press typing away, churning out lines continuously since the beginning of the

---

[69] JOHN FANTE, ASK THE DUST 78 (1939).

[70] EDMOND ROSTAND, CYRANO DE BERGERAC 133 (Brain Hooker, trans.) (1923).

[71] Ibid. at 132.

universe cranking away without even a recess for
silicone lubrication squeezed in between the gears

4. very very very very very very very very *very*
quickly – that is, at the rate of atomic vibrations – at
$10^{15}$ lines per second

plugging away

**Those are very efficient and nanoscopic
printing presses you've got there!**

5. if we checked their progress, we'd find that – so
far (from 14 billion B.C. to today) – they would
have printed 1/30 of 1% of the total number of
possible lines

So, get in line[72] you Aloysius Snuffleupagus[73]

---

[72] *I Walk the Line,* JOHNNY CASH, JOHNNY CASH WITH HIT
HOT BLUE GUITAR (Sun Studio 1956) (side B, track 3) (the
unique chord progression of which was inspired by backward
playbacks on a tape recorder while Cash was stationed in
Germany with the Air Force just a few years before my dad
was stationed there without so much as a tape recorder and a
pair of Rossignol downhill skis to cram into his Austin Healey
and wow the Austrian women with).

[73] (1971-) His sad and echoey-voice; his almond-shaped head,
his uncomplaining scapegoating for Big Bird's missteps; his
indefinite imaginary friend status (as being or non-being (even
after the Sesame Street kids played 'London Bridge is Falling
Down' with him that one time and the Snuffy-sized teddy bear
evidence was left behind that other time)); his eyelashes that
blinked like lunar eclipses, that that *that* was friendship and
Buffy Sainte-Marie was the first to see the light of it there,

You: hi-soy-sauce scrambled procrastinations

happy birthday mr. president super-grover

cleveland, ohio cryogenics, moon-rover,

angel-food-rattle-snow-melts,[74]

distorted poached zippers,

wrecked lampshades,

ketchupped buns,

prepositional

phrases

dots

**... *turning* toward something else**

---

beside the enormous nest in the urban alley. But the whole
unveiling of Snuffy was less golden as legitimate concerns
about widespread pedophilia and how children might get the
message (like Big Bird did) that no grown-ups would believe
their claims of reality and they were probably better off
keeping secrets to themselves. See also SNUFFY'S PARENTS
GET A DIVORCE (PBS 1992) (unaired).

[74] *I Melt with You*, MODERN ENGLISH, AFTER THE SNOW (Sire
1982) (side B, track 1).

*xl*

and

*Calvatias*  Puffballs of the whitest flesh
Which recall beefsteaks if
French-fried with cumin

*Lycoperdons*  Often found in half-shades,
Burnt-over lands, and rich woods
Try them baked in their own juice

*Amanitas*  Wookie growls[75] squared:
Its breath is fetid and sour
Its teeth thick and moist and mossy

*Pleurotis*  Sultry queens of phantom manure
Pink spores; overlapping filed caps
Sautéed like oysters, they melt freely

*Coprinus*  Freely forking on leaf-mold
*comatus*  If eaten raw, nutty and bitter
It has a shaggy-mane; it is inky

*Coprinus*  These – instead – are early-inky
*micaeus*  They adorn rubbish heads of spittle
Don't let their black juice repel you

*Clavaria*  A silver spoon against its skin
*pulchra*  Will tickle these club-shaped ones;
They prefer resting caves and poles

_______________

[75] Created by backward tape recordings of bear and walrus.

*Russula*        Orange-flecked globes which
*emetica*        Tell the best puns in the glade
                 If picked gently with temper gloves


*Morchellas*     Spongy, sweet, boxing-jocular
                 Typically located near sand-ponds
                 Or between the toes of ogres


*Fistulina*      Somehow, if squeezed with cream
*hepatica*       Into a muslin root ball over elk
                 Vinegar, these taste like osmosis


*Polyporus*      This testy fan-shaped sulfur one
*sulphureus*     Can be surprisingly tough so
                 Try it stewed with rabbit knees


*Lactarius*      Marked by concentric hues
*deliciosus*     The ousted-milk-mushroom
                 Is aromatic if baked correctly


*Cantharellus*   Its gills flicker and ripple
                 But only in the button stage
                 Its color? Dullest egg-yellow


*Hypomyces*      Funnel-shaped and heavy
                 Parasitic fungi with cute coats
                 Which taste like hail stones


*Marasmius*      Boasts convex caps, erect
*oreades*        In fairy rings; hundreds;
                 Leathery, they decay slowly[76]

---

[76] EUELL GIBBONS, STALKING THE WILD ASPARAGUS (1970).

but let's not forget our
satellite-island sitcom

decaying away on tv with this theme song

"Just log in now
as this yarn unspools
a yarn not lacking quips
which arcs up from this lunar port
on a chrome sub-light-speed ship

Consort: A 3ʳᵈ-rate sexbot lad
'The head' slicked back his fur
Their cargo blasted off to Mars
in a five-plank beam-split blur

A cosmic ray soon breached the hull
The head threw up his lunch
Were it not that the sexbot manned the helm
the *Arcus* would've crunched

Their ship smacked down on Deimos' cusp;
a spinning grey-black tar –

    With sexbot Dan…
    the fur-head too
    six cones of fuel…
    & their tanks
    the ra-di-o:
    Wrecked telemetry
    and booster pods

there on Silicon's-Chyle ♪

So, this is the tale of our characters
They won't survive six days
To give them hope and save their stuff
we made some games to play

The fur-head (Jim) and sexbot (Dan)
will perish where they rest
To live until some help arrives?
It's a lunar-lunchroom jest!

No cords, no lights, few $O^2$ tanks
A joke of a colony
Like ranch-style homes in Tuscon
it's primitive as can be

So, cluster 'round and place a bet
(Don't let the supers cheat!)
'Cuz fur-head/sexbot castaways
technology they can't eat"

*repeat* (indefinitely if one wishes to avoid the
German fascists) and if one doesn't then


*u try*
*turning*
*a page – when*


*fascism's <u>sticky</u>*

xlii

Nazis atop the moon cross-country skiing
across the lunar dust and out of a ridge, thus:

Cresting the top and hitching her gaiters
Elke peered past the Gagarin Crater

As she glassed clear 'round, her tripod folded,
into her vision, an astronaut strolled

The Nazi squinted – Was this day foretold
when the Allies were spotted on patrol?

Into her crosshairs nine hundred yards out
Jubilant in low gravity, he bounced

Inside her suit, the sniper's breathing slowed
She squeezed the oak-stock into her shoulder

Without so much as a 'pop' the man dropped
For a moment he quivered, then he stopped

Humming back homeward, her pace was a jaunt
Singing "All the Lebensraum We Could Want!"[77]


*Ugh!*

---

[77] To the melody of *Comme d'habitude*.

*xliii*

Humpty Dumpty – He was all thumbs
Serving, he tripped – 'Twas half past one
The other wait-staff told boss-man the truth:
"Uncle," they tugged at him, "Egg drop soup"

###

I'm sorry ♪ I'm sorry ♪ I'm sorry ♪ I'm sorry ♪ I'm sorry ♪ I'm sorry ♪

I'm sorry ♪ I'm sorry ♪ I'm sorry ♪ I'm sorry ♪ I'm sorry ♪ I'm sorry ♪

etc.

*"1-2-3-4-5*

*Once I caught an egg alive"*

*###*

*"6-7-8-9-10*

*Next, I let it go again"*

U.S. tax terms[78]

the 'gross estate'
shall include
the value of all property
to the extent
of the interest therein

of the decedent
at the time of his death

and the gross estate
shall include
any interest therein
of the surviving spouse

as dower
    or as curtsey

the term 'understatement'
means the excess
of ten percent of the tax
(or, if greater, $10,000)

or
    ten million dollars

the understatement shall be reduced
by that portion
of the understatement

---

[78] 26 U.S.C. §§ 2001 *et seq.*

attributable to

any item
if there was substantial *authority* ...

or

any item
       if there was adequate *disclosure* ...

and

if there is a *reasonable basis*
for the tax treatment
(by the taxpayer)
(herself)
while

the 'retention of the right to vote'
(directly or indirectly)
shall be considered
a 'retention of the enjoyment'

and the 'power to terminate'
shall be considered to 'exist'
on the date
of the decedent's
'death'

even though
the exercise
of the power
is subject

to
a precedent

or

even though
it takes effect
only on the expiration
(of a stated period)


(*this* 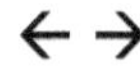

← →


↑stated
period)


and

*xlv*

an eucatastrophe @ Gilead[79]

Pruning hooks mincing
Hooves like flintlocks
Wheels like a whirlwind
Threshed and winnowed

She was not shrewd in-her-own sight
Like a tomb-terebinth, strong-as-oak
With its stump remaining in earth
For 7 ages after it had been felled

A sacred seed within her stumped;
Took heed; she thrust firm-in-faith
Her heart was not in the least faint
She was fastened as a peg securely

It was as deep as Sheol; thorns/briars
Someday we'll be eating curds there
The lord shaved with a razor hired
Far beyond a river's spoils; snared

She was *Maher-shantal-hash-baz*
Her tongue like a pen, threaded
Fragrant as myrrh, aloe, cassia
Stabs of labor spread like rugs

The sycamores were contour-felled
With cedar-bole cunit replacements

---

[79] RICKIE LEE JONES, BALM IN GILEAD (Fantasy 2009).

The bricks were fallen-down there
We'll dress stones in their places

They amassed us from the lip; none moved
Lest awards gather regrets from 1-fathered
None were crippled & remnants found return

Any child
can

write them
down

(*Selah*) Scrawl aloud a daughter

She scrawls:


## "*Please turn the*

*page*"

*xlvi*

Finesse

The charcoal patterns around

>    her chrome intake pipes
>    patterned like a good eye liner

No one taught an ocean liner to swim

>    she had to tutor herself
>    to win can you imagine

What might had passed

>    for lips were cracked
>    she seldom blinked

She was no commercial liner she

>    had forgotten more than
>    capitalists had ever known …

### 

Ferns                    Fiat Fuses

Ferociousness            Fraternities

Fluoride                 The Fragrance of Frogs

xlvii

Fancy *these* fins: a piece of fishcake

She takes the prize

She takes this sponge cake

She took it (the sponge cake, that is) on the run

She takes the area of any circle with a radius of one

She *holds* its top layer as if it was frisbee-fun

She maintains a flaky crust and spoons in dun

She owns a ratio of its circumference to its diameter's husband

Sliding it into her kindergartener's Hasbro EZ-Bake Oven®

It's as

easy as

3.1415926535897
93238462643383
27950288419716…

***Easy – Easy to turn…***

treading water cavity-free with sense perceptions

a shared popcorn society such as

a shiver up the spine = a proper hallmark of us
for Data ≠ cringe nor faint nor squirm in his seat

When robots develop a sense of the macabre
They'll have approached human equivalency

Dogs or chimps or dolphins might be disgusted
or repelled; but being *horrified* is so recherché

a great liquid squishing sound going 'plop' ♪ –
'plop' ♪ – something rising, unbidden; dark[80]

That's us in there making sense of it
making a horror of it; it's awe-full

the what-it-is which thralls us is not so much the
*what* but the *us* in it with it – or what we *mix* in
it, at any rate, with one single solitary exception:

## Spooky Trees

Even a $5 (U.S.) calculator shudders at their
branches framing a Halloween sky shrieking

---

[80] *Chicken Heart*, BILL COSBY, WONDERFULNESS (Warner
Bros. 1966) (side B, track 1).

###

lathed combustion chambers;
good old-fashioned adorable reason;
a poem or sixteen thousand of 'em that wouldn't fit
anywhere else; &

sure as heck wouldn't fit

here <sup>+</sup>

would they?

*Il faudrait des pages et des pages*[81]

---

[81] Tessa B., *Des Pages*, DANS MA TÊTE (Parlophone 2020) (track 7).

*Oui?*

xlix

We & St. Claire, whose fine-tooth comb[82]

    grained mahogany epidermis
    chafed under her two-sizes-
    too-small hypergolic igniter

    Each pound of medieval fuel
    kept; it steadied her up-ward

    Her bosom buzzed with a
    caravan of camels braying
    Nitrogen cups overflowing

    Camels of Midian; of Ephah
    She nursed at royal breasts

    She knew exactly where
    the salons were redrawn

    She was anxious for her exile
    'Mitts-off at lift-off,' she supposed
    a round sound; her aperture opening

    the front of her jacket, neat fasteners
    deliquesced, taking in the light breeze

    She didn't tie her own sash; she had
    been osculated by nimble burnings

    She would be escorted to a mountain

---

[82] See *supra* poem *i*.

97

where her enemies would lick her dust[83]

All of these contentions were liberating
her straight onto the straight-path-blast

She'd abvolate from blank edges of dark
and run a course clear across – skyward

silvery sprinklers on, slowing for a picnic
lunch, and taking delight in the highway


*Turn*


    *Turn*

---

[83] See *Dust in the Wind*, KANSAS, POINT OF NO RETURN
(Kirshner 1977) (side B, track 2).

*Turn but not*[84]

---

to hell with the signs passing by

one-by-one-by-one-by-one

sixteen-sixteen-sixteen[85]

tons

by which *L–* meant whatever is used in
signifying / two categories can be described:

*I*. <u>signs whose use consists in signifying</u>

and here of course is a set of examples laid

out on *this* ↑ ↑ ↑ ↑ ↑ line

| | |
|---|---|
| one of them is | "and" |
| another is | "here" |
| still another is | "of" |
| one more? of | "course" |
| a verb? an | "is" |
| and one | "a" |
| and a | "set of" |
| what? | "examples" |
| which were | "laid" |

on and so on

---

[85] To be read with an inflection signifying the skipping of a
record player needle.

*To everything*

*turn, turn, turn*[86]

**II**. and <u>signs which not only signify but also confer an interior aid</u>

    such as sacraments
    of the law

    such as vows
    and covenants

    such as ceremonies
    and blessings

admitting that all these signs are also things
quoting St. Augustine here: whatever is not a
thing is nothing at all; but it is not conversely the
case that everything is a sign; some things are
signs and other things are things they are

---

[86] *Turn! Turn! Turn (To Everything There is a Season)*, TURN! TURN! TURN!, THE BYRDS (Columbia 1965) (side A track 1).

things

of which *L–* explained – there are

three types:

***Primo***, those <u>*which* enjoy and/or use</u>

like us! (including Blake Sheldon, obviously)

and angels also

placed between the other two things
on either side of us and the winged ones:

***Secundo***, then, on <u>one side</u> of us,

high high high –

way up high

*so* high up on the cliff

the <u>things to-be-*enjoyed*</u>

[which, technically, are beyond the contest
of this sentence]

hardly even 'things' at all
and difficult to name suitably; semiotically –

though my personal fav tricky-to-name person
is "I Am Who I Am"[87] & if you ever meet a
gent at an office party with a --



name tag --

introduce yourself, bow, take off your flip-
flops and start figuring out how to get the hell
out of Egypt

such matters have been excluded from

*S is for Sentence*[88] and… while we're at it,
let's also exclude

      bobbleheads; and
      green jellybeans;

---

[87] *Exodus* 3:14. Get off the bus, forget about us, and hide
yourself in a cleft. Ibid. 33:22; *supra* note 44.

[88] © 2021, all rights reserved; for educational and devotional
purposes only.

all the restaurant placemats I
collected as a kid; broken nose
catacombs; parking tickets …

but we'll exclude YHWH as un-name-able
though to *enjoy* 'em (these miscellaneous) is
something entirely

different

and really *quite* name-able and pronounce-
able: *viz.* to adhere in love for its own sake &
rest there; divinity known by way of its
effects; effects in matter and in matter's

motion[89]

*Non?*

---

[89] See *Romans* 1:20 ("invisible things … being understood by
the things that are *made*") (emphasis supplied). See also THE
INVISIBLE MAN (Universal Pictures 1933). "Claude Rains was
*The Invisible Man.*"[*]

---

[*] *Science Fiction/Double Feature*, THE ROCKY HORROR PICTURE
SHOW (Ode 1975) (soundtrack) (side A, track 1). "Then at a deadly
pace *It Came from Outer Space*[†] and this is how the message ran…"
Ibid.

---

[†] IT CAME FROM OUTER SPACE[π] (Universal Pictures 1958).

---

[π] Story by Ray Bradbury.[††]

---

[††] (1920-2012).

---

He grew up in Waukegan.

---

*lii*

No,

Prokéimenon GO

Cantilevers of grace; end-shards extending
A radial outstretching finds Bethlehem
upon a stage of hovering posture

Starred fragments
Suspended fixedness
Camped vibrations jarring

them both      Spinning[90]

She turned and acknowledged the patterns
for many so feast-days thus spiraled; for their
remarkable gestures / such remarkable relations

be stilled      They

reached deep into
ribbon-coins tied to
the box of Octoechos

Together, they pulled out a canticle plum
Now they blinked at each other like camera
shutters / rotating, this altar substituted an *atleir*

the scenic      Word

---

[90] See *supra* note 31.

staged
for us
and it
in us

vocalizing like a 5-pointed Bob Seeger appearing in
a white-hot pop-up book prop in our Kmart[®]-
approved nativity scene –


    *There I am –*

       *Up on the stage*     .

       *Here I go –*

       *Playin' the star again*

       *There I go –*

*Turn[ed] the page*[91]

---

[91] *Turn the Page*, BOB SEEGER, BACK IN '72 (Palladium
Records 1973) (side A, track 5). Not to be confused with Pete
Seeger.

**Tertio**, then, there, on the *other* side of us, are
the <u>things to-be-*used*</u> – but never perversely nor
unlawfully

the world; the offered things created in it…
such things named and nameable alike

all their genera and units

negations | privations[92]
accidents[93] | essences

their unity | their existence

and to 'use' them is meant something also
name-able: *viz.* to place them in the power of
will; to apply whatever comes into one's
hands to obtain that which is to-be-*enjoyed*

For YHWH so loved matter[94] that he gave his
only…

---

[92] "The time has come for … Starvation / Excitation /
Femalization / The time is gone for … Desegregation /
Privation / Arf!!! Damnit." *One Day*, FISHBONE, TRUTH AND
SOUL (Columbia Records 1988) (side B, track 2).

[93] "Hey, it isn't accidental." *Hey*, JULIO IGLESIAS, HEY!
(Columbia Records 1980) (side B, track 1).

[94] LOUIS M. SAVARY, TEILHARD DE CHARDIN ON THE
EUCHARIST: ENVISIONING THE BODY OF CHRIST 16 (2021).

he gave his only sun … and YHWH thundered,

> "Here comes the son *doo-doo-de-doo-doo*"[95]

And YHWH yodeled,

> "*Whoa, whoa* – sweet darling
> (every night and day-ay!)
> You get the best of my love"[96]

And the choir caroled back,

> "Blinded by the light
> Revved up like a deuce,
> another runner in the night"[97]

And the people belted out to a party of three,

> "*Oooh!* did I tell you, 'I need you'
> Every – single – day – of my life"[98]

---

[95] *Here Comes the Sun*, THE BEATLES, ABBEY ROAD (Apple 1969) (side B, track 1).

[96] *Best of My Love*, THE EAGLES, ON THE BORDER (Asylum 1974) (side B, track 5).

[97] *Blinded by the Light*, BRUCE SPRINGSTEEN, GREETINGS FROM ASBURY PARK, N.J. (Columbia Records 1973) (side A, track 1).

[98] *Got to Get You into My Life*, THE BEATLES, REVOLVER (EMI 1966) (side B, track 6).

liv

such as the unwritten monographs of the late super-*super* great Lester Bangs[99]

A REASONABLE GUIDE TO HORRIBLE NOISE (1983)

A BOOK ON THE EVERYDAY LIVES OF PROSTITUTES, MOST OF IT WRITTEN (1996);

YOU CAN LIVE LIKE A BILLIONAIRE ON NO INCOME – I DO ALL THE TIME, AND THIS BOOK TELLS HOW (2004)

ALL THE THINGS YOU COULD BE BY NOW IF IGGY POP'S WIFE WAS YOUR MOTHER – A BOOK OF JIVE 'N' VERITIES (2011)

A ROCK VERSION OF A.B. SPELLMAN'S *FOUR LIVES IN THE BEBOP BUSINESS* FOCUSING ON BRIAN ENO, MARIANNE FAITHFUL, LYDIA LUNCH, SCREAMIN' JAY HAWKINS, ROBBIE ROBERTSON[100], DANNY FIELDS etc. etc. etc.[101] (2019)

---

[99] (1948-1982).

[100] Lead singer of The Band. See *supra* note 38.

[101] Greil Marcus, *Introduction & Acknowledgements*, in LESTER BANGS, PSYCHOTIC REACTIONS AND CARBURETOR DUNG xiv-xv (1988).

*lv*

Twelve drummer drumming ♪

Eleven pipers piping

Zen cords a-leaping…

### ###

100,000,000,000,000,000,000,000,000,000,000,000,
000,000,000,000,000,000,000,000,000,000,000,000,
000,000,000,000,000,000,000,000,000,000,000,000

bottles of beer on the vestibule ♪

100,000,000,000,000,000,000,000,000,000,000,000,
000,000,000,000,000,000,000,000,000,000,000,000,
000,000,000,000,000,000,000,000,000,000,000,000

bottles of beer

Take one down – Pass it around –

 99,999,999,999,999,999,999,999,999,999,999,999,
999,999,999,999,999,999,999,999,999,999,999,999,
999,999,999,999,999,999,999,999,999,999,999,999

bottles of beer on the vestibule, etc.

… that'll tie your ambo up for a while
                              that'll get you …

*lvi*

## Tied Up in Knots with

## Too Many Books and Garth Brooks usin'

A figure 8

A bimini twist

A butcher's knot

A girth hitch

A munter mule combo

A soft-shackle Edwards

A west country whipping[102]

A half-hitch

A clove hitch

A brummel splice

A grog sliding splice

A mcdonald brummel

A rat tale stopper knot

A whoopie sling

A sheet bend

An alpine butterfly bends

---

[102] *Whipping Post*, THE ALLMAN BROTHER BAND (1969 Capricorn) (self-titled) (side B, track 3); see also *Has Abolished the Pillory*, SPOKESMAN-REVIEW 6 (March 22, 1905) (taking note of Delaware's repeal of the pillory, a/k/a Whipping Post, a/k/a Red Hannah).

Introduction to Atomic Theory

directed by         the commander-in-chief
produced by         the military industrial complex
                    and;
*starring –*         in order of their appearance –
                    (…casting still in process…)


[title cards]


one anonymous 3.4-star general
 twin maids with flaming red hair
  3.1 diabolical demons as their foil
   6 staff with 4 matches in their teeth, a bombshell
   with radiation poisoning, a paladin with a
    redemption
     arc and …


<cue somber marching theme>

NARRATOR


"In a world
where governments
are infused with turning-the-world-into-a-cinder
in order to save it …"


CUT TO


Our dashing protagonist, pith helmet removed,
pearls glinting in a werewolf sun – his eyes angle
toward us – his smile broadens like a canoe

FADE TO

Chaos/screaming/alleyways/sirens/rainswept
concrete too hot for puddles to form upon

NARRATOR (Cont.)

"… one man is ready to do a little bit of *naming*,
and what greater *sacrilege*, he queried, to anyone
who would listen – than to heap unmentionables
upon icons and saints, stomp out the missals and a
few nuns, and just torch the *whole damn mess*?"

CUT TO

Hero roundhouse-punching a blonde wax-
moustached villain <pow!> in the jaw

[title card]

**R E S E T**

Coming Spring 2024

## Traps

Out of the fur trade and into the fire
Pliers walking trap-lines avoiding the briars
Daily checking on 'em; the toothy lyres the snares

the deadfalls / the trapping pits / the glue traps / the
body grippers / the foothold traps / the cubby sets

Like those Aborigines walking on and about

Blowing being into the holes of the bait

Bringing pink into the ark

some glow into the coals

The bloody red hats

torn by cranes

animistic

catches

swim

far

away from Lumellogno – some 3 hours and 40 minutes via A1/E35 southeast (angle downward at Milan; take a hard right at Bologna) – there lies Florence where Daniel Day-Lewis took a respite from acting in the 1990's to become a cobbler under the tutelage of Stefano Bemer[103] paying for the privilege with acting lessons so far as we know, so very far

---

[103] Stefano Bemer (1964-2012) crafted shoes for Julio Iglesias (b. 1943), among others.

"Away" was her name, the young cardiologist with
lester's bangs, birth pangs, penny-less penny loafers

She winked

and she whispered over the edge of a plaid daven-
port to me that her 'last lover' had 'been a poet'


and that 'made him more like a doctor'

and I told her *I* was '**more of a critic**' and

that made me '**more like an instructor**' then

she said, 'or a mortician' and I didn't laugh


and so, I tried, '… **or a chiropractor?**'

and that was another dead end

with nothing to commend


it because she didn't

understand any

of the modern

## Trends

like using Bruce Springsteen's
modems to one's own ends –

like investing it in Robin Hood
and watching it spend –

like bussing teens to private school
and watching them fend

for soon they'll be running out of guiles
to mend and

I'm running out of friends
to lend

to you rummaging about for more
rum to recommend

to a mechanic with whom I woke up
to the horror of pretend – and now

that I've got just one parent
to tend

I'm

running out

of

     Folks

"you've been
such a great audience

*I'd like to thank each and every one of you for
stopping by –*

thank you ♪ thank you ♪ thank you ♪ thank you ♪
thank you ♪ thank you ♪ thank you ♪ thank you ♪

thank you ♪ thank you ♪ thank you ♪ thank you ♪
thank you ♪ thank you ♪ thank you ♪ thank you ♪

[big gulp of air – *gulp*! and one sip of water – *sip* ]

thank you ♪ thank you ♪ thank you ♪ thank you ♪
thank you ♪ thank you ♪ thank you ♪ thank you"[104]

and … finally

---

[104] *Closing*, STEVE MARTIN, LET'S GET SMALL (Warner Bros.
1977) (side B, track 6).

your squat grunts   your groans, dear reader

## *Did you know that you are very strong?*

– which in          my way[105]
of thinking         are signs

which *L–* may       have overlooked


<u>signs which express</u> but neither signify nor
justify – and always truthfully – like punk rock
bellows brought on by tiresome poets like me

coming from within us-as-subjects like you
out of our mouths and out of our manly chests

Spelled out on the local diner's sign
Special today? rump roast and neon taters
And which might be further subdivided into
species like pepper, praise, our salty Sun Ra's

curses          cutscenes
laughter        thanksgivings
holiday         cooldowns
and this        page baked

in a pan and o!

---

[105] *My Way*, FRANK SINATRA, MY WAY (Reprise 1969) (side
B, track 1).

blood-curdling *yalps*! widows meet quick-sand –

and o!
sing it, lo
like Gordon Gano:

*I wonder what she would say*       *if I told her*

*If I told her – I felt*       *this way –*

*All I can do*       *is patiently*
       *pray, pray,*
       *pray pray*
       *pray*[106]

so, please ♪ please ♪ please ♪ turn the page

please ♪ please ♪ please ♪ turn the page

**please please please turn the page**

insert: [bass solo]

insert: [drum roll…]

<u>**This is it**</u>:

---

[106] *Please Do Not Go,* VIOLENT FEMMES (Slash 1983) (side A, track 3). Sadly, Lester Bangs died from health food poisoning the year before the release of the Violent Femmes' first album. See *supra* note 101. He was just thirty-three. *Supra* note 99.

– one Jewish girl's 'yes'

is beyond any measure.

*~ The End ~*

**That *was* it!**

*L–* does not get around to Mariology until Book III of *The Sentences*, but given the foregoing extended contrivance of his second sentence from Book I, I thought it might be worthwhile to return to *L–* and to quote from his own doctrinal collection of thoughts on *Panagia*:

> [A]fter the assent of the holy Virgin, the Holy Spirit descended upon her, according to the word of the Lord which the angel had spoken, purified her and prepared both the power to receive and the power to beget the Word of the divinity. And then the Wisdom and Power of the most high God existing in itself, that is, the Son of God, *homousios* or consubstantial with the Father, overshadowed her, like a divine seed. From the most holy and most pure blood of the same Virgin, he did not procreate, but created through the Holy Spirit, and joined to himself, flesh of our ancient mixture, animated with a rational and intellective soul. Therefore he is at once flesh, and once flesh of God: at once flesh animated with a rational and intellective soul, and once flesh

of the Word of God animated with a
rational and intellective soul.[107]

*The Sentences* are really quite captivating. They really are. As the foregoing block quote demonstrates, they're readable. They're inspiring. And they're arguably second only to the Bible if we're going to go about ranking the influence of Christian texts on the entire span of Christian history.

*L–* held a sort of monopoly over theological instruction for centuries. But his *Sentences* are so seldom – *too* seldom – read today. And yes, although I said "afterword," this last small point has consumed, instead, not one word after, but several – indeed, several *sentences* (ha!) after the end of the long poem. But that's kind of my point. And lined sentences *do* tend to end with them (points, that is).

Here, for example, is one such point. A point. Did you see it?

And there ✝

God bless.

---

[107] III LOMBARD, *supra* note 24 at 99, quoting John of Damascus, *De fide orthodoxa*, bk. 3.

*Well, look at that!*

*This is the end of the book*

---

[108] (1471-1528).

*And you were <u>so</u> scared*[109]

---

[109] Cf. JON STONE AND MICHAEL SMOLLIN (illus.), THE MONSTER AT THE END OF THIS BOOK 22 (1971).